001. Battle of the Locks and Keys

002. Norman knight and archers, 1066

003. Knight performing homage, 1100

004. Alexander 1st, King of Scotland, 1107

005. David, Earl of Huntingdon, 1120

006. Norman banner and armour

007. Seal of Henry I

008. Figures with morning star and mace

009. Seal of Richard Fitzhugh, Earl of Chester

010. Richard Fitzhugh, Constable of Chester, 1141

011. Richard I, King of England, 1194

012. Alexander II, King of Scotland, 1214

013. Knight armed with a martel, 1220

014. William Longespee, Earl of Salisbury, 1224

015. Spearman, man at arms, and slinger, 1250

016. Archer and crossbowman, 1250

017. Eudo de Arsic, 1260

018. Shield of Henry II

019. Sagittarius

020. Armed figure, seal of Adam de Hereford

021. Military figure in a cointise

022. Peter, Earl of Richmond and soldier, 1248

023. Robert Rouse, 1270

024. De Vere Earl of Oxford, 1280

025. Knight of the Montford family, 1286

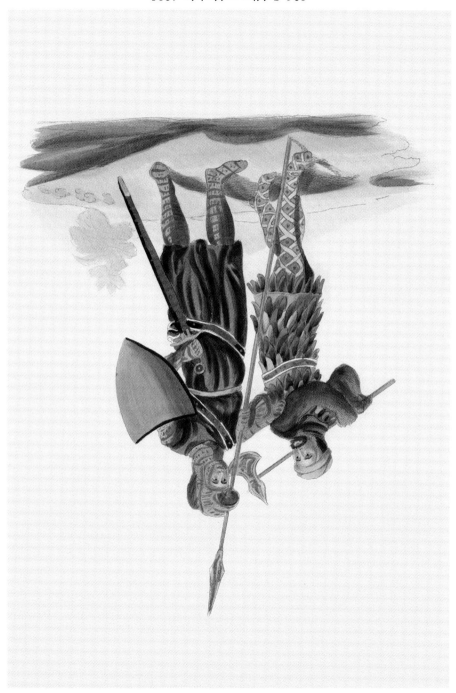

028. King and his mace-bearer, 1310

029. Archers and crossbowman, 1312

030. Aylmer de Valence, Earl of Pembroke, 1315

031. Knight, 1320

032. John de Eltham, Earl of Cornwall, 1329

033. Pourpointed armour with a tegulated pectoral

034. Edward II constituting
Thomas de Brotherton, Marshal of England

035. Edward III and the Black Prince

036. Combat between John Welsh and an Esquire of Navarre

037. Sir John d'Aubernoun, 1330   **038.** Sir Oliver de Ingham, 1343

039. Sir Guy de Bryan and Bernabo Visconti, 1365

040. Thomas Beauchamp, Earl of Warwick, 1370

041. Sir John Arsich, 1384   **042.** Knight of the Blanchfront family, 1397

043. Sir George Felbridge, 1400

044. Richard de Vere, Earl of Oxford, 1416

045. Knight of the Birmingham family, 1420

046. Thomas Montacute, Earl of Salisbury and a knight, 1422

047. A joust

048. Henry V being armed by his Esquires

049. Henry VI as St. George

050. Figure leaning on a pole axe

051. Henry VI, King of England, 1422

052. Two crossbowmen, 1425

053. Charles VII, King of France and Joan of Arc, Maid of Orleans, 1430

054. Crossbowman and his paviser, 1433

055. Richard Beauchamp, Earl of Warwick, 1439

056. Sir John Cornwall and Lord Fanhope, 1442

057. John Duke of Somerset, 1444

058. Sir Thomas Shernborne, 1458

059. Richard, Duke of York, 1470

060. Man putting on his armour

061. Richard III in his tabard

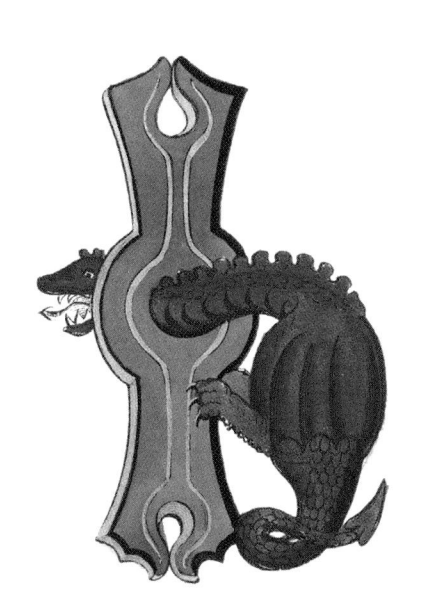

062. Dragon of Cadwalader

063. Figure from the target of Charles V

064. Sir John Crosbie and a sergeant at arms, 1475

065. Neopolitan suit of armour, Goodrich Court, 1480

066. Man at arms with a standard, 1483

067. Sir Thomas Peyton, 1484

068. Henry VII, King of England, and a billman, 1490

069. Maximilian I, Emperor of Germany, 1498

070. Sir John Cheney, 1499

071. Knight armed for the joust á la haute barde, 1512

072. Knight armed for the bond, 1512

073. Knight and one of the king's guards, 1525

074. Henry VIII, King of England, 1525

075. Black armour, 1534

076. Armour, 1540

077. Genoese armour, 1543

078. Long-bellied armour, 1545

079. Judith

080. Figure armed with a military fork

081. Halberdier

082. Pikeman and a swordsman

083. Armour, 1550

084. Group of soldiers, 1554

085. Armour, 1555

086. Federigo Oricono, 1558

087. Embossed armour, 1565

088. English gentleman, 1590

089. Bavarian suit of jousting armour, 1600

090. Officer of pikemen, 1616

091. Armour, 1620

092. Black armour, 1625

093. Harquebusier

094. Harquebusier and pikeman

095. Duke of Orleans wearing the gorget

097. Horse soldier and musketeer, 1640

098. Cuirassier's armour, 1650